Morgan is 20 years old and currently residing in Canada. He loves to write, paint, and read. He is currently working on his next poetry novel and enjoying the outdoors in his spare time.

I would like to dedicate this work to my family, and the people I'm still trying to understand.

Morgan A.L. Mel

SCRIBBLES

AUSTIN MACAULEY PUBLISHERS™
LONDON * CAMBRIDGE * NEW YORK * SHARJAH

Copyright © Morgan A.L. Mel 2024

All rights reserved. No part of this publication may be reproduced, distributed, or transmitted in any form or by any means, including photocopying, recording, or other electronic or mechanical methods, without the prior written permission of the publisher, except in the case of brief quotations embodied in critical reviews and certain other non-commercial uses permitted by copyright law. For permission requests, write to the publisher.

Any person who commits any unauthorized act in relation to this publication may be liable to criminal prosecution and civil claims for damages.

Ordering Information
Quantity sales: Special discounts are available on quantity purchases by corporations, associations, and others. For details, contact the publisher at the address below.

Publisher's Cataloging-in-Publication data
Mel, Morgan A.L.
Scribbles

ISBN 9781647506391 (Paperback)
ISBN 9781647506384 (Hardback)
ISBN 9781647506407 (ePub e-book)

Library of Congress Control Number: 2023920851

www.austinmacauley.com/us

First Published 2024
Austin Macauley Publishers LLC
40 Wall Street, 33rd Floor, Suite 3302
New York, NY 10005
USA

mail-usa@austinmacauley.com
+1 (646) 5125767

I would like to thank Austin Macauley publishers, for I've been wishing for this opportunity for a long time, and it means a lot to me to have a personal piece of my work regarded as a lovely manuscript.

Ugly?
Is that what you call yourself?
Abandoned?
Like a broken toy on a shelf?
Lonely?
Is that the word you moan?
Wretched?
I won't let you be alone.
Dying?
Like the life in your eyes.
Worthless.
Like all my lies.
Please don't love me
Just hold me
Just know me
Just kiss me
Just feel me
Just love me

I write under the cover of night
It is all I own
My only fight…
How would I have grown?
I had no shrink
Just my paper
And my blood for ink…

I know you are one of them
I won't leave.
One of the gone
You shan't grieve.
Slowly slipping from my soul,
These thoughts are wrong.
You'll be a mere headstone—
Please be strong.
—Laying dead behind my throne,
You shouldn't be alone.
I know what this throne truly is.
Tell me?
This is a rusty a cage.
Just break that padlock with me.
You will hate my rage.
I understand you.
I am stupid—
No.
—Under your age.
I understand you.
I wish you would
Let me in?
If only I could.
You have before
And never again.
I won't give up.

Just close this chapter.
No!
Just turn this page.
Don't be alone!
I know you will leave in time,
Never!
Once you see what lies beneath;
Lies!
All that bitter grime.
You can trust me.
I know I can.
Just give it time.

"What the fuck do you want?"
"Just to chat."
I rolled my eyes at her shrug.
"I can see that."
I expected a victimizing taunt.
But what did I get?
Arms awaiting a hug.
"Come on."
My palms were wet.
Her arms fell to her hips.
I rolled my eyes at her quivering lips.
"I'm glad we met."
"Why?"
My words were dull and dry.
"You can tell me how you feel."
"Why?"
"You know I always pry."
There came that smile.
The one I hadn't seen since I left her.
I abandoned her.
My poor, poor mother.
"You want feelings?
"Find my younger self,
"The boy with his drunken father,
"The boy all alone—
"Never comforted,

"Not in your arms of stone.
"I hated you then.
"When you tore my family apart,
"When you sent me to the wolves,
"And they carved out my heart.
"He made me hate myself,
"And you knew this would happen,
"I couldn't escape,
"That world I was trapped in,
"I tore through my flesh like paper,
"Forcing my tears to fade
"Away in the air,
"Like vapor.
"That was this world you made.
"I was but child support then,
"Fed on shitty scraps,
"And stolen booze from your den.
"I wish you knew,
"I wish you knew what I'd gone through,
"But I know,
"You would just make it about you."
"Son—"
"Shut up!"
I snapped at her.
She seemed ready to run,
The one thing she was good for,
That damn shell of a whore,
Clad in the robes of a nun,
"You thought you deserved so much,
"All you could do was take,
"And lie,

"You fucking fake,
"I will never know what is real,
"I was raised on your lies,
"'I love you,'
"'I'll protect you,'
"'I'm the victim,'
"Say now what you meant,
"'I'll use you,'
"'I'll instill fear within you,'
"'I'm the abuser,"
You fucked my mind,
I've had it,
I've had it with your kind.
You want me to love you,
You want to be worthy of that,
You want me to hear the shit you spew,
Maybe you want it to be true,
You can convince yourself then,
That you're worth it,
You aren't worth shit,
You want to know what I feel?
I feel something,
Like I have been stung by an eel,
But with this pain I can give thanks,
For at least I can feel.

Please,
Whisper after the screams,
Please,
Caress what has been bruised,
Please,
Make love to what has been raped,
Please,
Hold what has been thrown away,
Please!

I want it pouring out of me,
B
Distract me from this hell.
L
It's all I want to know,
O
I am so low,
O
That this may aid me…
D

'I won't leave you'
I've heard that one before,
'I love you'
I've heard that one before,
'I care'
I've heard that one before,
Please
I've heard it all before!

Just let the dust settle
Give me a home.
Don't make me go mental
I don't wish to roam.
Constance is so damn brittle
Give me time to think.
Can't we meet in the middle
Let's sit and have a drink.
All this movement is horrible
I just want something to stay.
Let it turn old a little
Let this fade to gray.
Please just let the dust settle
Please don't blow it away!

– White
I love you
I want you
I need you
– Black
I hate you
I want you out
I need no one
– White
Please hold me
Please listen
Please kiss me
– Black
You'll hurt me
You'll degrade me
You'll betray
– White
I trust you
I believe in you
– Black
I trust no one
I believe in no one
– White
Stay here
– Black
Go away
– White
Don't listen to him

– Black
Listen to me
– White
I'm sorry
– Black
That's right
– White
Goodbye
– Black
Get out
– White
Protect yourself
– Black
From us
– White
From him
I'll just expect them all to be you
I'll spend my life searching for that Joey tattoo
Or those beautiful eyes of bright blue…
How can you expect me to move on from you?
After the pictures on my heart you drew…
After all you have told me
And after all you knew…
After how much my love has grew
How do I move on from you?
I'll never love again
Once you meet your end
No one will have those beautiful eyes of bright blue…
Or that stick and poke Joey tattoo
I refuse to let go of you…

The sky must exist as a blanket over you
Like that hoodie and my vest there to warm you
That cool breeze there to soothe you
The blades of grass reaching out to hold you
Even the plants are mesmerized by those eyes of blue
That soft skin, cheeks with your pink hue
That smile, no matter how many times it's seen, it's new
And that captivating heart of blue…

It's a wall
A glass wall
Between you and I,
But you see
You exist
Unlike I,
You try
To convince me
To deceive me
But I…
I know
I died
Long ago.

How dare you say you love me
And be unfazed by my absence,
How dare you say you need me
And now tell me you never have,
How dare you say you know me
And not see,
This is my vulnerability.

I followed my favorite color down the road
So my favorite color could lead me to you,
Or your body…
I followed my favorite color down the street
So maybe I could wrap you up,
And save you…
I followed my favorite color down that path
Because my favorite color might lead to you,
Now I have no favorite color…

Want me to tell you why it's a mistake?
That rope will make your damn brain ache.
Want to know why you shouldn't do it?
Have you ever heard your seeping skin slowly split?
Want to know why you shouldn't die?
Drowning will make your fucking lungs fry.
You know why you'll live?
Because you can still try.

I want health
I've survived too many times,
This is it!
Maybe this is my ending.

You asked why it didn't work?
Why I didn't cut deep enough?
Why I didn't drink enough?
Why I didn't take enough?
Why the rope wasn't tight enough?
Why I didn't stay under long enough?
Why I managed to eat enough?
You expect some profound response
Some beautiful words from a tortured mind
You do not understand how I can want death so bad
And yet to my body I am too kind,
I've searched forever
Hope is not what I will find…
I've no idea what keeps me here,
Why I am trapped
Stuck in this world of fear…
And every day death is coming
And what can I say?
I say; "Come here"
Why hasn't he answered?
For I have made it clear…
I hate this place
I do not wish to be here
So to answer your question;
"Torture, my dear."

I burned with you
I lit that match
Knowing my skin would catch –
Knowing I would be set ablaze
By your touch
Your feral gaze
I can't comprehend this
How we can part ways
I burned to ash for you
I felt hell's flame
I knew it was you I would never tame
That in every lifetime we play –
We play this unholy game
But even as I burn
I find euphoria in these flames…

I tried to leave when I saw what you were,
You wouldn't let go
You hurt me for her…
How could you hold me down and bleed me?
How dare you call me your enemy
I begged you to loosen your grip
Let me take one step back,
And for my throat you went for the attack…
I loved you and you bled me dry,
You kept me in your rotten cage
Then spat on me for making you cry…
And why?
Why is it always retaliation that makes your blood fry?
You can't abuse someone
And then question why they don't care if you die…
You told me to leave if you scratched my skin
And for that
Where do I begin?
You hurt me to help them
Sanctimonious wannabe saints coated in my blood and yours,
It's still those demons you adore…
All I wanted was for you to hear me out
Believe my accusations
But I didn't deserve the benefit of the doubt
In your eyes I was the villain for biting back…

How could I have shown respect after the attack?
After the belittling?
The alienation?
The dehumanization?
The degradation?
But this is what you expected of me
To be a punching bag yet again
But not just for you
But now for them
It isn't even you who makes me sick,
It isn't even those little pricks—
It's me!
For searching for light in the dark
Using water to make a spark
Yet again thinking a killer could smile,
Not letting myself think your heart was selfish and vile…
For letting the holder of cyanide make my tea
And will I ever do it again?
Most likely…
I treated you how you treated me
And for that you shot me in the knee
And what does that say about you?
About me?
Do you say you deserve this injury?
And why do I fight back?
When do I go home to my shack?
Lay up my hat
and put away the bat?
For you will never understand what you are
We all know you're worthless
So why show you by telling you

You'll just cut our throats
You'll figure it out when everyone leaves you
For then you can see no person
Just your lonely reflection…
And your dead eyes
And you'll know
I told no lies…

Everyone wants the tortured writer until they see what is bred by torture
Until you see the empty bottles
The wounds you can't nurture…
The anger we harbor
You come for the roses
The beautiful words
The kisses in the rain
Those white birds…
But will you stay when you see the pain
When you find the blood drops in black ink
When you see it isn't all beautiful
When you see every artist has a hideous canvas
That they close their eyes when they pass
Every writer has a depressing book
To which they cannot even give a look…
Every singer has one song that hurts to sing
It makes their ears ring…
Beauty has to come from pain
The loveliest eyes have burning tears
The most complex brains have the strangest fears…
And if it is those things you can love
If these hideously beautiful things entice you
You must be wonderfully broken too…

I want to set my brain on fire
For it is still you I desire…
After you watched them hurt me
I should have busted knees…
You sided with someone who pulled on a rope around my throat
No, I should cut your heart out
And for that I'll gloat…
You gaslighted me for a pedophile
You should have busted knees
You're pathetic
You're vile…
You're a repugnant piece of putrid filth
I hope they hurt you next
Then you'll know guilt…

She's a part of me
A part unknowing of love
Of glee
A part that's only felt skinned knees
Blood knuckles
Broken bones
But no heart to own
Just this lonely thrown
She's a part of me
A part that has not grown
A part that hates to be alone
She wants to love
She wants to be hugged
He's a part of me
Into the deepest pits he's dug
He won't move
Won't even make a shrug
Uneeding of eyes
Unhearing of lies
He's a part of me
The part too scared for cries
He's here when innocence dies
Alone and feral
He's finally escaped his own hell
She's a part of me
Her voice rings like a bell

She sits in her room alone to think
Surrounded with walls of pink
In love with the thought of love
She's part of me
Hearing screams from above
Trapped in these white walls
Her arms forever cradling her chest
He's a part of me
Your worst is his best
He's skinned completely
Burning in hell
Writhing and screaming
Trapped in his cell to fester
He's a part of me
We just call him monster
And this is my family

How do I stop myself from getting close?
How do I stop myself from trying to love?
How do I stop myself from needing someone?
How do I stop being hurt?

Would you call me a poet?
I'm just bleeding onto paper.
Would you call me an artist?
I'm only trying to dull the pain.
Would you call these words lovely?
I just use them for the wounds I taper.
Would you say this is healthy?
This is when I started pouring my booze down the drain.
Or would one say I've gone insane?
For the delusion that this keeps me sane.

I was six at the tenth time of losing everything
Stuck in that hell,
Hearing screaming and death threats
Just waiting for the bell…
I think I was seven when you locked me in there—
With no food
And I created the girl with the black hair….
I was eight when you scorned me
It was in a way I could never understand,
So, I listened to your command…
I was thirteen when you tied me to you,
You fucking pig!
Into hell I hope they throw you…

I tried nightly for a week to end my life
I've used a noose
A bathtub
A knife
I lost it all
My home
My pet
My lovely lowlife
Now what am I left with?
My life

I hate this agony
I hate that I saw it
I saw it reaching for me
I saw you stab me
And smile with glee
Then you threw a fit
The second you saw me bleed
You were all I could need
And you threw me in this pit

Oh, Aphrodite!
Bring them to me
Oh, Aphrodite!
Please fill my heart with glee
Oh, Aphrodite!
Strike joy into my heart
Oh, Aphrodite!
Don't let us be apart
Oh, Aphrodite!
I was born to stare into their eyes
Oh, Aphrodite!
You know my lips can't form lies
Oh, Aphrodite!
I will love them eternally

There's this constant back and forth
It's burning through my mind
There is no closure—
No way to unwind.
Should I miss you?
Should I hate you?
Should I be glad you're gone?
Should I cry for doing wrong?
It was the both of us
It was you
It was me
Who the fuck was it?
Why can't I be free?
Why must these inner battles plague my brain?
When will this end?
When will I know the truth?
Is there a truth?
It's not like either of us won
We died in blood after having so much fun.
Am I right either way?
Am I wrong either way?
Who's to say?
It doesn't matter, anyway.

What the hell is wrong with you?
How could you care after the blood I drew?
Why is it me you wish to find?
After looking in my rotten mind?
Why do you wish for my time?
It should be a crime!

You just threw me out
Into the cold,
Alone!
My heart is in a drought,
You hurt me
And you let them hurt me
And I didn't even doubt
Our love—
Our connection!
And I still crave your affection…
I still burn for those awful words
They were like acid in my mouth
I still pray for your attention…
You said you wouldn't care if I died
You spit on me as I cried…
Why do I still wish for you to see?
See how they treated me
See that you belong in my arms
See that I will repay doing you harm…
I still wish to work on us
I don't want to give up on you
Despite how ugly this grew…
I still hope that you think of me
Sitting at your table
With a cigarette and a coffee
And I still think of you…

Re-watching that garbage movie
Quoting those stupid lines to me
You still warm my heart
And for this I will forever be torn apart…

Every fucking poem I write is about you
Every fucking song I sing is about you—
What about me?
Do I even exist without you?
You were a part of me
For such a short time,
But you've left me forever changed
I don't know where to start—
Should I move on?
For it looks like you're gone
Or should I wait?
My heart knows that you're my fate.

I can feel this aching
This throbbing…
Like my heart is breaking –
Shattering –
I can't stop shaking
I'm crying
Someone end this panicking…

This world doesn't feel real
Not in the slightest
How do you heal?
When you can't breathe
And when you can't feel
I was to feel
Any emotion
Do I drink?
Do I steal?
It doesn't help
I can't think.
Someone shut of my brain
Or reduced it to a tiny grain,
Swept away by the ocean
Taken
Like my emotions,
I've become robotic
My skin feels too thick—
Too heavy
Like metal

I'm terrified
Mortified
My brain is fried
I wish I had died
At least I can say I tried

How do I tell you I'm not all in your head?
How do I tell you our love is real?
You belong in my bed,
I'll hold you while you heal…
You say you can't forget us
Then stop trying
You can surrender,
We have this flame
Something so tender…
We've tried to be tame,
But we're pulled together
So come with me
And embrace our flame…

Why did I drink the poison?
Why did I hurt myself?
Why did I look at your picture?

I want to crack open your skull
I want to look inside –
Inside your mind
I want to know why you did –
Did those awful things
I want to know why you liked it
I want to know why it was so euphoric –
So euphoric that you risked your life to kill
I want to meet that monster in your mind
And I want you to meet mine!

They're after me
The men in the trees—
They'll kill me
They're out to get me
The men in the trees—
They can hear me
They put thoughts in my head
They want me dead
I can hear them in my head…
They're out to get me
Nowhere is safe
If I run,
I'll be chased
If I hide,
They'll hunt me down
Rip off my gown,
And rape me
They're after me!
The men in the trees

I want to be on fire
I want to burn
It's my desire,
To touch it
Feel the fire,
Feel it eat at my skin—
Until nothing is left
But the meat once within,

I'm still in that room…
Without food
Without water
I can't get out
This is my doom…
I can hear my blood
It's coursing through my veins
The only voice in this room…
The only thing without pain

D
They're here with me
I
To hold me when I cry
D
They won't leave me

I can hear you
Why did you do?
Where did you go?
They found out
I know that they know
You need to hide
Stay inside!
I won't let them hurt you.
I won't let them near us.
Just listen to me
See what I see!
For we have the key

They're not after you
I promise
You're safe for today
They're not after you
I promise
They won't take you away
They're not after you
I promise
You're here to stay
They're not after you
I promise
Let your fear decay
They're not after you
I promise
You won't go astray
They're not after you
I promise
You're safe

Take off the hospital gown,
Remove yourself from that place
You'll lose your fear
Your frown…
Come here, my dear!
You can trust at your own pace
You'll lose your fear
Your frown…
Come here, my dove!
Let yourself know love

Jail is my mind
Useless is my body
Sullied is my soul
Tainted is my heart
Fucked is my future
Undeserving is what I am
Careless is what I have become
Knives are my only wish
I need them
No other way
Give them to me
Kill me
Ill me
Ll me
L me
Me
E

I'm trying to get better
I promise.
I've put down the knife
I promise.
I don't drink
I promise.
I stop and I think
I promise.
I try
I promise.
Did you know?
I lie.

I can't stop thinking about you
Fuck!
Just kill me
Shit!
I need a lobotomy

Can you just touch me?
Just to lessen my agony…
I need to hear you sing,
Their screams still make my ears ring…
I need you here,
I need you near…

I love you.
I promise!
No matter how stupid I get—
I promise!
I love you.

"I don't want to kill you."
It meant, "I love you."
To her
"I didn't burn the pictures you drew."
It meant, "I care."
To her
"For you I won't go to the chair."
It meant, "I won't hurt you."
To her
"I decided not to tear out your hair."
It meant "I love you."
To me

I want to see you,
In the cards
Your name
Your aura
I want to see you,
In the cards
With me
Madly in love,
Forever!

You wouldn't understand!
What happened that night
The screams and endings and revenge and betrayal
You wouldn't understand!
The anger that took flight
The rage and happiness and promises and safety
You wouldn't understand!
If I brought this to light
The secrets and pain and tears and trauma
You wouldn't understand!
Not tonight

This dark night
It houses this fear
Gripping my throat
Squeezing the life out of me
Popping my eyes out of their sockets
Someone tell me you're not in pain
I need to know
Or this hand with remain
Gripping my throat
Choking me to death
I can't breathe
I can't move
I can't think
I am frozen
Lifeless
Dying
Please be okay
Make the hand go away

There's bottles all over the floor
What has he done?
To make you not want me anymore—
I want to keep him away
I have such little time
For him to be at bay…
Please lie to me
Tell me you'll stay…
After you meet him
Tell me you can tell us apart,
I am not him
For I have a heart…
It beats
It pounds for you,
Regardless of what he's said
Screamed
The things he threw
I'll keep him away
I promise
My heart belongs to you…
Yell back
Bring out the tortured boy,
He won't say those things
You're not his toy…
I promise
We can find away

If you be with me
If you just stay
Look past those red eyes,
Into my ocean blue
Turn away from his lies—
You know I love you
No matter what he says
You know my heart is true
It beats for you
I know your heart does, too…

Let me rekindle!
I know I've done wrong
I've known it all along
I was just scared
That fear poisoned me
Don't you see?
You've struck to the heart of me
Let me show you!
I have grown
I can be your phoenix
You're all I've ever known
Let me love you now!